Let Us GIVE THANKS

ROBERT PERKINS

ARPress
ILLUMINATING IDEAS.
EMPOWERING VOICES

ARPress
45 Dan Road Suite 36
Canton MA 02021
Hotline: 1(800) 220-7660
Fax: 1(855) 752-6001

Ordering Information:
Quantity sales. Special discounts are available on quantity purchases by corporations, associations, and others. For details, contact the publisher at the address above.

Printed in the United States of America.

Library of Congress Control Number
ISBN-13:   Paperback   979-8-89389-049-5
                            eBook   979-8-89389-050-1

Rev. date: 4/3/2019

Contents

Introduction ix

Giving Thanks for a Good Job... 1
Giving Thanks for a Pleasant Day 2
Giving Thanks for a Power Source 3
Giving Thanks for a Promise Kept 4
Giving Thanks for a Surprise.. 5
Giving Thanks for Adoption... 6
Giving Thanks for Archeology 7
Giving Thanks for Art... 8
Giving Thanks for Beautiful Music 9
Giving Thanks for Books to Read 10
Giving Thanks for Childbirth...11
Giving Thanks for Competitive Sports.. 12
Giving Thanks for Computers 13
Giving Thanks for Dreams 14
Giving Thanks for Education 15
Giving Thanks for EMTs 16
Giving Thanks for Encouragement..17
Giving Thanks for Entertainment 18
Giving Thanks for Every Saint 19
Giving Thanks for Fairy Tales 20
Giving Thanks for Heavenly Sunshine 21
Giving Thanks for God's Forgiveness...22
Giving Thanks for Guardian Angels 23
Giving Thanks for Freedom Fighters... 24

Giving Thanks for GPS 25

Giving Thanks for Greeting Cards 26

Giving Thanks for Furniture 27

Giving Thanks for Foreign Lands 28

Giving Thanks for Heaven 29

Giving Thanks for Flatware & Dishes 30

Giving Thanks for Insurance 31

Giving Thanks for Laughter 32

Giving Thanks for Local Zoos 33

Giving Thanks for Love and Romance 34

Giving Thanks for Mentors 35

Giving Thanks for Museums 36

Giving Thanks for New Glasses 37

Giving Thanks for Nursing Homes 38

Giving Thanks for our Friends 39

Giving Thanks for Rainbows 40

Giving Thanks for Precious Gems 41

Giving Thanks for our Phones 42

Giving Thanks for Restaurants 43

Giving Thanks for our Pains 44

Giving Thanks for Revivals 45

Giving Thanks for Science 46

Giving Thanks for Simple Farms 47

Giving Thanks for Smiles! 48

Giving Thanks for the Bond of Love 49

Giving Thanks for the Comforter 50

Giving Thanks for the Disabled 51

Giving Thanks for the Fire Department 52

Giving Thanks for the Four Seasons 53

Giving Thanks for the Games We Play 54

Giving Thanks for the Gift of Death 55

Giving Thanks for the Law..56
Giving Thanks for the Moon and Stars 57
Giving Thanks for the Police Force 58
Giving Thanks for Time..59
Giving Thanks for Time With God 60
Giving Thanks for Vacation...61
Giving Thanks for War & Peace...62
Giving Thanks for Warmth 63
Giving Thanks for Wedding Days..................................... 64
Giving Thanks for Wheelchairs..65
Giving Thanks for Gods Word... 66
Giving Thanks for Our Home...67
Giving Thanks for the Great Outdoors 68
Giving Thanks for Our Physicians 69
Giving Thanks for the Breath of Life 70
Giving Thanks for Our Children...71
Giving Thanks for God's Wisdom.......................................72
Giving Thanks for Our Freedom 73
Giving Thanks for Our Health 74
Giving Thanks for the Gospel 75
Giving Thanks for Therapists 76
Giving Thanks for Missionaries..77
Giving Thanks for Our Technicians 78
Giving Thanks for Clothing and Food 79
Giving Thanks for the Ministry 80
Giving Thanks for Gravity..81
Giving Thanks for Beautiful Flowers 82
Giving Thanks for a Good Nights Rest...............................83
Giving Thanks for Our Pets 84
Giving Thanks for Medication 85
Giving Thanks for Mom and Dad.......................................86

Giving Thanks for Our Veterans 87
Giving Thanks for the Gift of Prayer.............................. 88
Giving Thanks for Our Tears 89
Giving Thanks for Christmas 90
Giving Thanks for Easter Day.....................................91
Giving Thanks for Thanksgiving 92
Giving Thanks for Memories.......................................93
Giving Thanks for the Lord Our God..............................94
Giving Thanks for a Home Church.................................95
Giving Thanks for Transportation 96

Introduction

Why did I write this book on giving thanks? Because I don't think people thank God enough for what they have been blessed with.

But let me start at the beginning: Linda, my wife and I, had noticed one day that the local retailers had skipped Thanksgiving when it came to their seasonal advertisements. I said, that isn't right! Thanksgiving is as important as any other holiday, if not more so. So let's see what kind of things I can give thanks for in poetry form. For one month, I penned poetry: at least 40 or more poems on what I thought important. Then I put the project on hold.

I didn't do anything with it until about five years ago, when I completed the book. I hope you find this eye-opening, especially about the little things we take for granted.

I know I've left a lot of things out of this book. If you can think of more reasons to give thanks, send me your ideas, and who knows, a second volume may come of it. It's all up to you.

Enjoy!

Robert Perkins

Giving Thanks for a Good Job

Some people hate to go to work
They'd rather call in sick, or hurt,
  But they pull themselves out of bed
  They have to work for their daily bread.

Then there are the other folks
Who are pleased where they must go,
  It's a joy to work amongst friends
  Even when the day seems to never end.

That money that fills their pocketbook
Pays the bills, and buys them food,
  Sometimes they even get to go out
  An extra that blows away their frowns.

Thank You, Father, for places to work
May we enjoy them, sharing your word,
  Jesus, You blessed us with something to do
  Let us do it wholeheartedly for You!

November 21, 2014

1

Giving Thanks for a Pleasant Day

On a walk amongst the trees
You are cooled by a delicate breeze,
    The clouds drift by far up above
    Without a care, almost as one.

Some fellas like to sit and fish
Taking their time; there's nothing like this!
    Painting or drawing, to bide their time
    To share their gift is a true delight.

God sends along these pleasant days
To shower on us undeserved grace,
    Ah, that blessing from heaven above
    Is returned to Him by giving Him my love.

Holy Father, I thank You again
For this day that's about to end,
    Jesus there were no storms today -
    Thank You for this pleasant day.

November 21, 2014

Giving Thanks for a Power Source

The sun looks down from the heavens above
Smiling down on us with Gods love,
    Bestowing his power on the good and the bad
    Melting clouds like ice in a desert land.

Another power source comes from below
Oil that needs refining, don't you know,
    Oil becomes gas, or petrol some say
    To run our cars, trucks; any way we play.

Windmills are another source
To brings us a new source of fuel, of course,
    Just because it hasn't been proven
    Doesn't mean it can't be used then.

Holy Father, You created all things
You are the Power, above all dreams,
    Jesus, You are the Son of Our God
    Thank You, Lord, for all that we've got.

November 18, 2014

Giving Thanks for a Promise Kept

Trust comes from a promise kept.
For some it is a lost concept.
    To keep ones word, to do what is said
    Does not bring doubt but faith instead.

Some people cannot fulfill their word
They want to be true, but their word is impure,
    Who can trust them if a promise is broken?
    They walk away, sad, and heartbroken.

A promise kept brings hope indeed
Hope and faith, integrity, peace,
    God Himself made promises to man
    None could be broken, they are part of his plan.

Father God, the Promise You made
Was to send Jesus in our place,
    Jesus You fulfilled what Your Father said
    And became the hope of a Promise kept.

December 3, 2014

Giving Thanks for a Surprise

Surprise! Surprise!
Who wants to live a boring life?
    Now and then things come along
    That shake us up; hit us sidelong.

The same old thing isn't good for us
Dance a jig! Take a new bus!
    Do something daring, far beyond you
    Stretch yourself; you might like the new you.

Surprise, surprise! God has a plan
That involves every woman and man,
    It may not be evident, but you never know
    You may leave behind an eternal glow.

Thank You, Father, for little things
That enliven our souls; oh how they sing!
    It was a surprise, Lord, when You came down
    To live among men, without Your crown.

December 8, 2014

Giving Thanks for Adoption

Some women just cannot give birth
Oh, they want to, but it won't work.
>   That is why they do it this way
>   To fulfill their desire to be a mommy.

I know of a family in my church
Who had to adopt; she could not give birth.
>   Now that they are a happy family of four
>   Will they possibly adopt any more?

Adoption is an act of God
Sharing His love with those who have not,
>   Whether man or woman, as they search
>   They want to share Gods love so pure.

God adopted us into His family
The day we accepted what happened to Jesus,
>   Jesus you are more than our friend
>   We became Your family. Amen.

December 2, 2014

Giving Thanks for Archeology

Children have the right idea to dig
They might discover something big!
    Their parents say no, so the children stop
    When a few feet away was the big 'pay off'.

Men and women grow up with a dream
To hit it rich through archeology.
    They sign on with a discovery team
    And give it their best - to fulfill their need.

They may not find something right away
It's just the challenge, not the pay.
    If something big does comes along
    Their heart can sing a joyous song.

Father, You know what's hidden out there
And You know who will find their share.
    Archeologists dig and search, Jesus Christ
    Trying to find it at the highest price.

December 5, 2014

Giving Thanks for Art

Fine art, Abstract, impressionist too
All through the ages were created by you,
    You reached down and touched their hearts
    And that is where creativity starts.

You are the Artist who out performs all
You grant the gift, and still stand tall!
    In six short days You created all things
    And even today your creation sings.

Penmanship, painting, planting a seed
Are forms of art, established by Thee,
    Who can outshine Thee? You are the one
    Who created Jesus, Your sinless Son.

Father, paintings and sculptures remain
To share with others how You create,
    Jesus, our talents flow from inside
    Because our praise we cannot hide.

November 26, 2014

Giving Thanks for Beautiful Music

Styles and styles of music today
From classical to the country way,
    R&B, Rapp, Christian too
    They even have one called the Blues.

For each person there is a style
Something that soothes them for awhile,
    Some bands fill the soul with power
    Passion that stirs them by the hour.

Christmas hymns bring me peace
What moves you may not move me,
    That is what unites each one
    Individual lives, individual loves.

Father we thank You for music, today
From rock and roll to a symphony,
    Jesus let us give to You
    The glory and praise due to You!

November 15, 2014

Giving Thanks for Books to Read

Other places, other times
Mystery books, or books of rhyme,
    Romantic books that take us away
    Or devotionals that make us pray.

Giving thanks for books to read
Is fulfilling to each of our needs,
    Some folks love to feast without fail
    On historical fiction, or a sci-fi tale.

Then there's the humorous side of things
We laugh until our heart sings,
    All considered, books feed our mind
    From children's books to important finds.

Thank You, Father, for the printed page
That fills our souls nearly every day,
    Thank You, Jesus, for your Book
    The Holy Bible - it's worth a look.

November 19, 2014

Giving Thanks for Childbirth

After nine months of growing inside
It is time to come out, explore the outside,
    In the hospital, the labor pains start -
    Now they aren't too far apart.

Oh the pain! Can I bear it?
Here she comes, here is Sarah.
    Hold her tenderly in your arms
    Hold her closely to your heart.

Were the birthpains worth it now?
Yes they were, oh and how!
    To see this baby in my arms
    Is a miracle, so helpless and warm.

Father, your Son was once like this
In a manger, so tender, being kissed,
    Jesus you were a tender Child
    Who lived with us for a while.

December 2, 2014

Giving Thanks for Competitive Sports

Does this sound like 'games' to you?
Nothing could be more from the truth.
    There are the Olympics, soccer, rugby
    Baseball, football, and so many others.

These rough and ready competitive sports
Have one thing in common, the final goal!
    To win the game at any cost
    Without the possibility of failure or loss.

One on one the players give
Of themselves until they win!
    That's what makes this competitive sports
    It's not a strategic game on a board.

Father, sports can be a tricky thing
But in the end, we want to win and sing,
    Jesus no one wants to fail You
    But if nothing else, we'll take No. 2!

December 2, 2014

Giving Thanks for Computers

People might question this idea
Of lifting our thanks, but think about this -
 Without computers how would we fare
 Without iPad, iPhone, so many that are out there.

We correspond with computers these days
I'm using one this poem to create,
 They assist kids in doing home work
 Whether at school or using Microsoft Word.

The world is changing at a rapid pace
Either keep up, or get lost in the race.
 Computers are evolving almost every year
 That you'll get lost in the past is my fear.

Father, how did computers come about?
Should we praise them, or have our doubts?
 Jesus, they're here, so how do we use
 These computers we have to glorify You?

December 2, 2014

Giving Thanks for Dreams

Dreams are seeds of a creative mind
Inventions grow from dreams that fly!
    Take for example, the Wright Brothers idea
    When others said no, they took to the sky!

Someone designed the first computer
Now those computers are everywhere.
    Don't give up. Keep seeking your dream
    And one day soon it could become real.

Reaching out to the universe
Is beyond my dreams, but they're doing it now,
    Dreams are just waiting to be attained
    Time to step up and make a claim.

Father, you bless us with all kinds of dreams
Some are small, some are big,
    Jesus, inspire us to accept what You send
    And use our dreams to the very end.

December 5, 2014

Giving Thanks for Education

Public schooling vs. home schooling?
Any education is better than no schooling!
    But with violence in schools today
    It's become a challenge to educate.

Public libraries are a treasure indeed
For those who wish, and love to read,
    Computers are now educational tools
    Being installed in all, or most of the schools.

Colleges, universities, the local church
Bring opportunities for us to learn,
    God has blessed us with inquisitive minds
    Let us fill them with educational light.

Thank You, God, for the thirst to learn
Even from the Bible, Your Holy Word,
    Thank you Jesus, for instructing nations
    With Your Fathers love - education.

November 23, 1997

Giving Thanks for EMTs

When we need an emergency ride fast
911 is our best bet,
　　EMTs arrive in minutes
　　To take care of our broken limbs.

They take us to hospital admittance rooms
Where we're transferred to ICUs,
　　From there we are examined by the best
　　To go upstairs or home to rest.

EMTs are there to serve
When we can't do it on our own,
　　Let us give them thanks tonight
　　For how they daily save our lives.

Father, we thank You for these EMTs
Who give of themselves so selflessly,
　　Jesus, You stopped to heal so many
　　Those who were sick, now have a'plenty.

November 29, 2014

Giving Thanks for Encouragement

Sometimes life can be a drag -
Pull yourself up by your bootstraps!
    You need someone to help you up
    To dust you off, and give you a hug.

Encouragement comes in many forms
A smile, kind word, a hand shake so warm,
    Are you one to give your love away
    To encourage others by kneeling to pray?

Lift them up with a compliment now
Even occasionally take them out,
    You never know when you might touch
    A soul that needs it oh so much.

Father, we thank You every day
When You hear us as we pray,
    You encouraged us, Lord Jesus Christ
    By becoming our sin sacrifice.

December 7, 2014

Giving Thanks for Entertainment

We watch them perform on TV or stage
They entertain us every day,
    Is it comedy or drama, tonight?
    Or suspense that leads us to fright?

Then there's the art festival every year
It's free to the public - people still cheer!
    When they pass the hat at intermission
    To make their goal, they are wishing.

For many years entertainment's been there
To bring us joy, wash away our cares,
    Let us thank those who are in the know
    That we enjoy it, where ever we go.

Father we thank Thee all throughout time
For the joy we receive, whether prose or rhyme,
    Jesus You are the Creator of all
    Thank You for entertainments call!

November 26, 2014

Giving Thanks for Every Saint

After accepting Jesus Christ
In to the heart of our life,
    We become saints from that day on
    For our old ways are withered and gone.

True we may wander once or again
Into our dirty old lives of sin,
    Once we repent of what we've done
    He restores us by His love.

In the instant that we were saved
The Holy Spirit makes us saints,
    He sealed our souls with Jesus blood
    A seal that cannot be undone.

Thank You Father for calling us saints.
We are now holy via Your restraint,
    By Your blood we are bright white
    Saints once stained darker than night.

December 7, 2014

Giving Thanks for Fairy Tales

We dream of a place beyond this earth
Where fairies don't lie, they are pure.
> They have been known to seek revenge
> But it all works out for good in the end.

Sweet little girls dream these dreams
To dress up as a princess, a fairy queen,
> Little boys dress up as champion knight
> To save the princess in an evil fight.

Fairy tales can take us away
To a land where it's good to play,
> Give thanks to God for these tales
> Where nobility wins, dragons are impailed.

Holy Father, thank You for this
Land of the pure, a kingdom of bliss,
> Jesus, I pray that heaven will be
> 10 times as great as the land of the fairies.

November 20, 2014

Giving Thanks for Heavenly Sunshine

I know this overlaps just a bit
With the pleasant day poem I did,
    And yet I must say sunshine does more
    It feeds the flowers, and our spirit's restored.

As people sit beneath its rays
They try to turn another shade!
    Heavenly sunshine brings energy
    Which some people call vitamin D.

Is it true sunshine brings joy?
I'll take a truckload if that's so!
    To fight off the winter time blues
    I'll take sunshine, if that's true.

Father, You created the dark and the light
And saw it was good, that it was 'fine',
    Jesus, sunshine is more than good
    You are the Light that came to the world.

November 26, 2014

21

Giving Thanks for God's Forgiveness

Oh how hopeless we would be
If God's forgiveness hadn't set us free!
    The sins that held us like a vice
    Were washed away by Jesus Christ.

All we need do is accept His gift
By repenting of our sins.
    It's that simple, but some turn away
    Saying "Oh come on! Is there another way?"

Once we're forgiven, our sins are gone
Our soul rejoices with a heavenly song.
    We no longer want to live in the past
    But to live for God, whose kingdom's so vast.

Father, we thank You on this day
For washing every sin away.
    Jesus, had You not died for us
    There would be no forgiveness.

November 22, 2014

Giving Thanks for Guardian Angels

Unseen guests within your life
They stay with you both day and night,
    They protect you from unseen danger –
    These holy beings are Guardian Angels.

They whisper in your inner ear
The wisdom of God you were meant to hear,
    Angels leave it up to you
    To act upon the word of truth.

Look to the Father, thank him again
For these unseen angels he has sent,
    When you feel that unseen nudge
    Act upon it, it comes from above.

Father, we thank You for the angels around
Who watch and keep us; your love abounds!
    Jesus when you were in deepest need
    Angels were sent to minister to Thee.

November 20, 2014

Giving Thanks for Freedom Fighters

Hidden by grass or high in the trees
These men or women are there to bring peace,
    They have come to teach a new way
    Of living known as Democracy.

Men, women, children too
Could vote, or peacefully attend a school,
    For years this was only a distant dream
    But now it is more than a possibility.

No rights for women, children have less
Freedom fighters are there for them,
    To right the wrongs these people endure
    To start a new life, minus tanks and mortars.

Father, we thank You for those who come
To share Your peace from Heaven above,
    They may not come in Jesus' name
    But peace is their ultimate aim.

November 24, 2014

Giving Thanks for GPS

There was a time not long ago
When men wouldn't ask where to go,
    Whether traveling to a different state
    Or to watch their kids play games.

They knew that they would get there 'soon'
While others knew they'd get there past noon.
    So, when GPS appeared in most cars
    Relief sprung up in many hearts.

Now many guys find their ways
To their final destinations!
    No more lost ways, or being so timid
    To ask their way with a GPS.

Father, Your children wandered 40 years
Because Your law they did not fear,
    Jesus, Your followers have been blessed
    By keeping Your law, their GPS."

November 28, 2014

Giving Thanks for Greeting Cards

Why give thanks for greeting cards?
They can say what we cannot.
    Whether it's birthday, holiday, or lighthearted love
    Greeting cards say what we're thinking of.

Sentimental, silly, all kinds of words
Can lift you up with just the right verse,
    Send a card to those growing up
    Shower their day with all kinds of love.

Shower your friends with joy-filled praise
To lift them out of the bluest of days,
    When they get the card you've sent
    You may receive a call from them.

Father, You sent a card to us
A beautiful card filled with love,
    Your holy Bible, and Christ your Son
    Are greeting cards that invite us home.

December 6, 2014

Giving Thanks for Furniture

Here's one to make you consider
Where would we be without furniture?
    If not for chairs or sofas we'd sit on the floor
    Like our relatives of far far before.

Bookshelves, desks, China cabinets
We use them but we take them for granted,
    Beds and pillows help us to sleep
    Unlike the shepherds who tended their sheep.

They slept on the grass, the fertile ground
We have all types of furniture - look around,
    If we are not blessed, I don't know who is
    Give thanks to God, it is all His.

Holy Father, we are rich indeed
Thank You for the furniture we use and need,
    Jesus, You had not a pillow for your head
    You can have mine if You need it, my Friend.

November 20, 2014

Giving Thanks for Foreign Lands

We think they're strange, but no, indeed
They aren't the ones, but it is we!
    We are visiting in their land
    To diversify ourselves, to expand.

Cultures, languages, music, art
Take it in and become a part,
    A part of their daily life
    And soon it will feel to you just right.

Fact is your ways will come to be
What you once considered a need,
    We were the ones to understand them
    That's why we give thanks for foreign lands.

Father, God, You sent us away
To the four corners of Earth, one day,
    Jesus, You united us in foreign lands
    Which is why we give You thanks.

November 17, 2014

Giving Thanks for Heaven

Beyond our dreams, our mortal minds
There is a homeland so refined,
    It's streets are gold, it's beauty rare
    We can't see it, but it's there.

It is described in the Bibles last book
It is breathtaking if you care to look!
    Those who are saved will share their lives
    And their eternity with Jesus Christ.

We will sing our praises to God
We won't weary, we won't stop!
    Heaven will be our glorious Home.
    We will not move, we will not roam.

Oh holy Father, when Jesus comes back
We will disappear in the Rapture,
    Thank You, Jesus, for our home above
    Homes You designed out of pure Love.

November 25, 2014

Giving Thanks for Flatware & Dishes

I don't think I am going too far
By giving thanks for dishes and flatware.
    What would we eat off of, or cut our meals?
    Bark from trees, or sturdy leaves?

Laugh if you must, but consider the thought
Give thanks for all these blessings from God.
    Somebody created the very first dish
    And now you buy them whenever you wish.

Handmade or plastic, there they are
Or fine china, state of the art,
    So enjoy the many designs out there
    Some modern day, some quite rare.

Father, we thank You for the fact
Of dreams of dishes and cutlery/flat,
    Jesus, You knew our prayers and wishes
    And sent the idea for flatware and dishes.

November 25, 2014

Giving Thanks for Insurance

Here's a no brainer for some in the bunch
Insurance, to many, is a must!
    Should something occur that you don't expect
    Insurance is there to save and protect.

When our valuables are stolen away
By insurance we will be repaid.
    Should a loved one leave this world
    Their demise should be covered.

If a wreck causes you pain
And it wasn't your fault, give God praise!
    Insurance will be there to watch over you
    Like a big brother who sees you through.

Holy Father, You are safety indeed
By Your insurance we are freed!
    By your blood, Jesus, You broke the bond
    Insurance indeed that we are one.

November 28, 2014

Giving Thanks for Laughter

Laughter lightens the burden you bear
It takes away troubles with lighthearted care.
    Laugh at a joke! Tickle a child!
    Be the light of the party for a little while.

Laughter has been proven to relieve stress
If it is true we should all be blessed!
    Do you think Jesus frowned very much?
    Or did He laugh like the rest of us?

Go outside, run in the wind!
Race with the butterflies, they just might win!
    Laugh with the angels, sing like a lark!
    This is where laughter gets its start.

Father, You laugh with us every day
For those who fail You, You still love Your saints,
    Jesus You laughed with those who yearned
    To be more like You from what they heard.

December 4, 2014

Giving Thanks for Local Zoos

Since we cannot travel there
Zoos take us there for a minor fare,
    'There' being a foreign land
    Where exotic animals take a stand.

Australia, Africa, the frozen North
Are home to many animals of sport,
    But zoos defend these endangered species
    By taking care of their every needs.

People walk past them every day
In awe of their size and ferocity.
    Why do we travel to the zoo?
    To see what God can and will do.

God, You are the Creator of all!
To see Your work fills us with awe.
    Jesus, we see You, wherever we look
    At the zoo, or in Your Book.

December 4, 2014

Giving Thanks for Love and Romance

Walking along in a dreamy mist
Holding hands, making a wish,
    A wish to live forever as one
    It would be great if that were to come.

Enjoying a picnic in the park
Packing things up before it gets dark,
    Sharing a kiss (the very first one)
    Treasuring it forever with the one you love.

Standing up for your loved one in a fight
Not running away, or taking flight,
    Fight for her honor, let her know
    That you will love her wherever you two go.

Heavenly Father, You love us too
Perhaps not romantically that is true,
    But You love us enough that You would die
    And overcome sin, as You rose back to life.

November 15, 2014

Giving Thanks for Mentors

Life has many types of guides
To be a mentor is the very best kind,
    Leading the young down the narrow way
    Comes by time on your knees to pray.

Mentors, masters, those who teach
Instruct their apprentices under their wings,
    Then one day as they become of age
    They can earn a living, a wage.

The most important mentor of all
Is the Holy Spirit who breaks down the wall,
    The wall of ignorance falls as we read
    He fills our heart and mind with His seed.

Thank You Father for Your children who come
Desiring to be fed by Your grace and Your love,
    Jesus, how wonderful it is to be
    Saved and mentored by the Holy Three.

December 16, 2014

Giving Thanks for Museums

Some museums protect fine treasures
Others display worldwide pleasures.
    There were suits of armor that valiant men wore
    As they fought for their kingdom while at war.

Other things you might find on display
Are reproductions of the Wright Bros. plane,
    Egyptian art that goes back in time
    Depicting their unknown daily grind.

A few museums have a T-Rex
Meeting the folks as they enter or exit,
    Museums can be a fun place to learn
    With new discoveries at every turn.

Thank You, Father, as we travel these floors
Where we learn from Your stores!
    Jesus Christ, you hold the keys
    To our knowledge and each museum.

November 27, 2014

Giving Thanks for New Glasses

Without my glasses, I don't see much
But with my new glasses I see a bunch!
   Can you imagine not wearing a pair?
   In Christ's day there were no glasses to share.

If we now need to strengthen our eyes
Or we need an appointment to remove a stie,
   We go to the doctor as quick as we can
   And leave our problem with 'the man'.

New glasses correct our vision just right
Whether we are near or far sighted.
   To walk out of his office seeing quite well
   Brings joy to our heart and soul.

Thank You, Father, for glasses that change
And focus our vision in so many ways,
   Jesus, you touched and healed blind eyes
   Thank you for the miracle of modern day sight.

December 4, 2014

Giving Thanks for Nursing Homes

They're not as dreary as they once were
There might be a few, or so I've heard,
    But the ones I know of are very nice
    Especially the one that takes care of my wife.

Some people take their loved ones there
Then hope for the best nursing home care.
    They don't know that visiting too
    Will lift the spirits of their loved ones, too.

They believe the nurses can do it all
I visit Linda with weekly calls.
    Her MS is slowly stealing her away
    The best I can do is to visit and pray.

Father, I thank You for nursing homes
They are there when we can do no more.
    Jesus, You care for those who are ill
    Thank You for people who will do Your will.

November 22, 2014

Giving Thanks for our Friends

In a day where 'self' is in
It's a relief to know we have friends,
    Almost like family, they share our lives
    Becoming closer than family at times.

We laugh, we cry, we embrace and jest
Friends stay with you, when others have left,
    Reminiscent of a siblings bond
    They may quarrel, but are never gone.

Secrets shared, lives enhanced
Let us thank God for the gift of friends,
    Without friends, its a lonely world
    So next time you see one, tell them so.

Thanks be to the Father Above
Who gave us friends to share His love,
    Thanks to the Son, Jesus Christ
    Who is our best friend, throughout all time.

November 24, 1997

Giving Thanks for Rainbows

There's nothing better on a rainy day
Than when the clouds roll away,
    Leaving behind a sunny sky
    And a rainbow way up high.

When that rainbow does appear
From end to end it brings us cheer,
    It looks as if it's a painted arch
    - it is created by the Holy Artist.

Actually it's a covenant from God
Never to destroy the world by flood,
    So when you look up after a storm
    And see a rainbow, thank the Lord.

Thank You, Father, for the beautiful sight
Of a rainbow high in the sky,
    Thank You, Jesus, for placing it there
    And looking down on us with loving care.

November 15, 2014

Giving Thanks for Precious Gems

Unless you're rich you see very few
Precious gems; they are hidden from view,
    They glitter and gleam in jewelry shops
    Drawing people's oohs and ahhs!

One of these days they won't be rare
They will be common in Heaven, so fair,
    Gems like rubies, emeralds, garnets
    Will be worn next to our hearts.

Precious gems are hard to find
That is why they are the precious kind,
    Searching and seeking this type of gem
    Makes them more precious in the end.

Father, we know that heaven bestows
Beauty unheard of here below!
    With streets of gold, and mansions on high
    Prepare us, Jesus, for each new surprise.

December 7, 2014

Giving Thanks for our Phones

Once upon a time, long long ago
Believe it or not, there were no phones,
    To communicate then, we had to write
    Then give our messages a slow horse ride.

Things have changed since that day
Now we dial people up; they answer right away,
    We are connected for the most part
    By computers, landlines, emails, or cells.

Giving thanks for phones, you ask
Is that good, or is that bad?
    Well, it is if we're needed right away
    It's possible a life could be saved.

Father, we thank You for connecting us all
With a phone, whether landline or cell,
    Jesus, I know another way
    To get results, and that is to pray.

November 18, 2014

Giving Thanks for Restaurants

Whether gourmet, or fast food joints
Let us give thanks for restaurants,
    There are a few who cannot cook
    So off to these places they often look.

The problem is, if they come here much
It becomes evident in their pocketbook,
    Not only there, but in their waist
    Where they begin to put on weight.

I ought to know, that was me
Until I cut back on the 'feed',
    Still, now and then as I go out
    I enjoy a good restaurant.

Father, I thank You for people who cook
This is their art form from Your book,
    Jesus You sent them that we might enjoy
    The fruit of their labor - oh boy, oh boy!

November 26, 2014

Giving Thanks for our Pains

Inner strength comes from bearing pains
Pains that would steal our peace away,
    Look to the Lord, and lift your heart
    This is where true healing starts.

If you must, seek other help
God gave us doctors to make us well,
    Have all your friends pray for you
    Then believe that's all you must do.

Pray. Have faith. Know God is there
And that for you, He constantly cares.
    You are one of His children, you know
    Be strengthened by Him; off the pain will go.

Father, thank You for Your healing touch
Strength will come to us from above,
    Jesus, You may not heal us right away
    But, in time, You will ease our pain.

November 24, 2014

Giving Thanks for Revivals

No one wants to think they need help
But sometimes our soul is not well,
    We need replenishing, we need renewed.
    What it was like when salvation was new.

Revival picks up, where your soul was cold.
The Holy Spirit takes up control.
    Joy rings out! Hallelujahs ring!
    Renewed souls for the King of kings!

Blessings, blessings everywhere.
Those who held back, now don't care.
    Praising the Lord matters the most
    Joining in with the revival hosts.

Holy Father, take over again
Renew our hearts from the burden of sin,
    May Your praises flow from our hearts
    With revival that your Holy Spirit imparts.

December 8, 2014

Giving Thanks for Science

To understand every thing there is
Or how it came it in to being,
    Is the key to the study of science
    And where it could take us in this life.

Was it creation or evolution
That set every thing into motion?
    Will evolution end it all
    Or will a nuclear bomb be the final call?

There is so much to know and learn
From the scientists here on earth.
    To them, new discoveries thrill their soul
    Which is what living is all about, you know.

There are those who study You, God
But science, Father, is what they call it.
    Thank You, Jesus, for those who seek
    To know You better - starting at your feet.

December 5, 2014

Giving Thanks for Simple Farms

Driving past farms, we don't think
How much work and upkeep,
    There is in that little farm
    That is so cute and has such charm.

Every day they milk the cows
They feed them too, and slop the sow,
    When time is right they plant corn and wheat
    And harvest it for us, to enjoy and eat.

The meat is sold at the county fair
To keep the farm running, and more to spare,
    That's just the beginning of what goes on
    In the farm You smile upon.

God, we thank You for those who plow
And give more than they return somehow,
    Jesus, You know how this farm was run
    Bless them and keep them as a family of one.

November 16, 2014

Giving Thanks for Smiles!

Smiles brighten up a dreary day
Especially those on children's faces,
    Joy that radiates from heaven on high
    Brings peace and love to a soul that cries.

Wake up friend and smile again
If you don't have a smile, look to a friend,
    They will gladly share one with you
    And pull you up out of the blues.

It doesn't sound like much I know
Giving thanks for a beautiful glow,
    That's where smiles originate
    From the soul, to melt away hate!

Father we thank Thee for a gentle smile
May we return it to others for a while,
    Jesus, He smiled on all of man
    Now, may we return it and call Him our friend.

October 30, 2014

Giving Thanks for the Bond of Love

We meet a girl, some handsome guy
And we fall in love, there on sight!
    We buy our rings, say our vows
    Bonding ourselves in love - wow!

An over-simplification of the events, I know
But it is something most of us do,
    God, on the other hand, forms the bond
    Which keeps us both faithfully in love.

Have you thanked God for the bond of love?
None can create it but the One Above!
    Let us thank Him for this gift
    That bonds life to life, as long as we live.

Holy Father, thank You, today
For the bond of love, which you create,
    Messiah and Lord, strengthen that bond
    To last, we pray, our whole life long!

November 23, 1997

Giving Thanks for the Comforter

The day of Pentecost brought a change
The Holy Spirit came to stay!
    He sent the disciples forth in the world
    To share Your love to those who'd not heard.

He comforted the weary, forgave their sins
By drawing the sinners unto Him,
    The seed was sewn, the word grew in their heart
    The harvest was great, from the very start.

Modern day students of Your Word
Are fed by the Comforter, the Counselor,
    This is how our heart and faith grow
    By inner peace, and the Comforter's glow.

Holy Father, Your Spirit came
To teach Your one and only way,
    Jesus I pray what the Comforter sent
    Will stay long after we repent.

December 8, 2014

Giving Thanks for the Disabled

Why give thanks for those who can't walk
Or those who cannot see, or talk?
    If you look closely you will see
    The courage it takes to get out each day.

I know a lady who cannot see
But she gets around like you or me!
    She has not given up on life
    Even without the gift of sight.

Another young man cannot walk
And yet his musical knowledge is off the wall!
    I could easily tell you more.
    So when you see them, pray for 'em.

Father, you created no mistakes - not one
Help us to reach out to the disabled in love.
    Jesus you did the very same thing
    By reaching out to them, as King of kings!

December 3, 2014

Giving Thanks for the Fire Department

We don't think of them until it's too late
And we have to call them right away!
    Then they rush to our homes
    To save us from the flames - oh no!

Remember these people in your prayers
We could lose it all if they weren't there,
    These fire fighters risk their lives
    By dowsing the flames, whether day or night.

They are committed to save as much
As they can, when all is done,
    These men and women put out flames
    So we can get back to our life once again.

Father, we thank You for people who save
Where we live with water they spray,
    Jesus we thank you for those who were called
    By fighting the flames that endanger us all.

November 23, 2014

Giving Thanks for the Four Seasons

Spring is gentle as all is renewed
Flowers, trees, your little heart too,
    Summer heat helps the plants spring forth
    Causing the crops in the fields to grow.

Come Autumn when all withers away
The beauty is there; most of it stays,
    Then when winter comes in to town
    All turns white like a frosty ghost town.

All four seasons must come and go
We may not see it, but it's there you know,
    They blend together, and then disappear
    To return once more, in another year.

Holy Father, you had this planned
These four seasons as a help to man,
    Lord Jesus, storms come and they go
    But if we lean on thee, off they will go.

November 16, 2014

53

Giving Thanks for the Games We Play

Why give thanks for the games we play?
Because they make us concentrate,
    The simple game of checkers, you see
    Makes you think of how to compete.

Chess is a high strategy game -
How do I play without a checkmate?
    Games, even fun ones, like playing cards
    Fill our time, when we have a down heart.

Euchre, Bingo, 500 Rum
Stretch our minds till the game is done,
    When the game's over, we are still friends
    It doesn't matter who loses or wins.

Father, we thank You, for the games we play
May people see You when we lose with grace,
    Jesus, we thank You for conquering death
    What the devil thought was a sure bet.

November 19, 2014

Giving Thanks for the Gift of Death

"Have you lost your mind?
"Why be thankful for death, tonight?"
    If it weren't for the gift of death
    We would never get to see Heaven.

Death is our release from this life
That we may be in the Presence of Christ,
    Our life, as we know it, suddenly ends
    And a glorious new life in eternity begins.

As we can see death's not a trap
But an open door to Freedom, at last,
    Stepping through, holding His hand
    Free's us from the trappings of man.

Our Father, we lift to You our thanks
For the gift of death You grant,
    Jesus, You faced death and overcame it
    Help us do the same with Your grace.

November 23, 1997

Giving Thanks for the Law

It all began at Mt. Sinai, long ago
Where God gave Moses His holy law,
    I won't tell you what they are
    Most of us already know them by heart.

And yet, have you noticed that modern laws
Sound like the ones of long ago?
    Murder, adultery, stealing things
    Are occurring on our streets.

Not much has changed, yet we must
Change our hearts, accept God's love.
    If we don't He will judge our ways
    So mind the Law, and pray, pray, pray.

God, You gave us the Law that we might be
More and more just like Thee,
    Yet, Lord Jesus come live in our hearts
    That where Your Law is it will never depart.

November 22, 2014

Giving Thanks for the Moon and Stars

The stars and the moon are mysteries still
To see their photos gives me a thrill,
    Far far away are gaseous clouds
    Not black and white, of multiple colors.

The moon has no air to breathe
Its powder won't support either you or me,
    But God created it as well as Earth
    He knew what He was doing, that's for sure.

To give thanks for the stars and moon
Is to thank God for His throne room,
    The stars are diamonds glittering high
    In His crown way up on high.

God, our Father, You created it all
From the Earth, to things that bring awe,
    Jesus, we lift our voices in praise
    For the moon and stars at the end of our days.

November 17, 2014

Giving Thanks for the Police Force

When things get rowdy close to you
There's one thing you need to do,
    Call the police to settle things down
    So you can have peace for a while.

The police who watch your neighborhood
Are there to protect you, do you some good,
    They will break up drug parties
    And arrest them so you can have peace.

As long as you remain anonymous
Revenge won't come when they get out.
    Police watch over us deep in the night
    When we are sleeping, unaware of our plight.

Father we thank Thee for those who serve
In the police force, or the reserve,
    Jesus we thank you for those who strive
    To keep us safe both day and night.

November 23, 2014

Giving Thanks for Time

What is more important today
To watch a game, or take time to pray?
    Time is given to every one
    How we use it is up to us.

Every person is blessed with time
Some live longer, others short lives,
    I hope that God calls me His friend
    By spending more precious time with Him.

I would rather read Gods Word
Than keep up with this wicked world,
    Redeem the time for when He comes
    He will call His beloved ones home.

Father mine, one of these day
Time will stop; You will call us away!
    Jesus, You designed everything right
    Including the very concept of time.

November 30, 2014

Giving Thanks for Time With God

Taking time out to study Gods word
Can open your mind to things unheard.
    You may have read the verse before
    But the Holy Spirit says 'Read it once more.'

Reading or praying; time spent with God
Is more than worth the time you've 'lost',
    You are feeding your eternal soul
    Or taking your needs to the One in control.

The more you read, the more God says.
Set time aside, even if it's in bed.
    Give God the best part of your day
    And He will bless you in all kinds of ways.

Father, teach us straight from Your word
What You desire from Your children on Earth,
    Jesus, as we spend more time with You
    May we desire to always be true.

December 6, 2014

Giving Thanks for Vacation

Ah, finally, the day has come
To take the family on vacation!
    The work's been hard, the hours long
    For two short weeks we can go have fun.

North, South, East, or West -
On which coast will we be blest?
    Something out there bares our name
    As we plan on getting away.

We must go soon, or use up time
Meant for us to ease our minds,
    Vacation time is precious to many
    So go, relax, use every penny.

Holy Father, thank You so much
For every vacation spent in love,
    Jesus, You spent many years away
    From Your kingdom, our souls to save.

November 29, 2014

Giving Thanks for War & Peace

War is caused by those who disagree
Some are shot, some fight, then some flee,
  Once the war is being fought
  Peace is the least of their thoughts.

Someone's right, someone's wrong
That is all that matters to them all,
  They are here to prove their way
  And if they must, they'll die for the faith.

When peace comes, as it eventually must
The soldiers rest, but think of Gods love,
  They remember the fallen, the wounded, the dead
  Without them peace wouldn't count in this land.

The war was fought by You, my Lord
And Satan lost, by a great majority,
  Thank You, Jesus, for the Peace you bring
  In to the life of a child of the King.

November 20, 2014

Giving Thanks for Warmth

We take it for granted on wintery days
That heat will surround us in every way.
    Warmth surrounds us; inside of a store
    Or in a car, with friends galore.

In the bed beneath a quilt
We cuddle up as if we might melt.
    Think of those folks out on the street
    Who would give anything for some heat.

This is not to make you cry
Just a poem to open your eyes,
    God has blessed us in so many ways
    Shouldn't we thank Him for heat, with praise?

Father, we thank You for the gift of heat.
How can we share it with those in need?
    Jesus Christ, change our ways
    As to how we can share our heat, each day.

December 5, 2014

Giving Thanks for Wedding Days

After months of romancing the one
Who thrills your heart, the time has come,
 The time to vow that you want them as
 Your one and only guy or gal.

Wedding day plans have got to be right
The pure white cake, the dress of white,
 The groom to be must give up
 His partying days for the one he loves.

Now as one, they bond their lives
As a betrothed man and wife,
 Soon there will be a number three
 To make this a beautiful family.

Holy Father, this is how You
See the Church, as they come to You,
 We seek our Savior, our Groom, Jesus Christ
 To be our beloved for the rest of our lives.

November 16, 2014

Giving Thanks for Wheelchairs

When I met Linda she was in a wheelchair
It was the only way she got from here to there.
    With assistance she could take a few steps
    Now she can't do that due to her MS.

Honestly, this is not a rhyme about her
Today I'm giving thanks for wheelchairs,
    Think of how hard it would be
    If there were no wheelchairs to set them 'free.'

Not only wheelchairs, but scooters too
Make folks mobile, when their feet say no.
    Give thanks to God for the person way past
    Who designed the wheelchair to get around at last.

Holy Father, You are the One
Who created the idea out of pure love,
    Jesus, You healed the body and heart
    Which is where true healing starts.

November 22, 2014

Giving Thanks for Gods Word

Let your fingers do the walking today
Through each and every sacred page,
    Pages filled with knowledge and truth
    Stories known by heart since youth.

The Holy Bible can be read or heard
A document that is God's holy word,
    Let us give thanks for this treasure trove
    And it's Author for making it known.

Yet in the wealthiest nation on earth
Few rarely read God's Almighty Word,
    Few of us give thanks for God's precious gift
    By returning to, and learning from it.

Lord, we would be far richer today
If we'd read your word, and pray,
    Today we thank you with heart and soul
    For the wisdom found in the Holy Bible.

Giving Thanks for Our Home

By the fireplace, in a cozy nook
In our bed, or reading a book,
    A 'home' is a precious place to be
    Even if your home is on the street.

Home is where the heart is, they say
Whether in a mansion or down on Main,
    God's been good to the known and unknown
    By blessing us all with some type of home.

There are those who still ask God
'Why must I live out of this box?'
    A better home is awaiting us someday
    So why not thank God instead of complain.

Thank you Lord for each of our homes
For the love that dwells in each one,
    It's not a house that makes it a home
    But God's love within it and that alone!

Giving Thanks for the Great Outdoors

Whispering winds through the trees
Soothing sounds of gurgling streams,
    The sleek look of a gentle fawn
    Or majestic colors of a brand new dawn.

Rain forests, oceans, mountains tall
Graceful rivers, they fill me with awe,
    The animal kingdom with lion as king -
    Let the hymns to their Creator ring!

As we camp out in a National Park
May we take its beauty to heart,
    May we remember that it was the Lord
    Who first created these great outdoors.

Lord God, we thank you as we pray
For the great outdoors which you create,
    We thank you Lord for its splendor
    Which you created with a few simple words.

Giving Thanks for Our Physicians

Broken limbs, ailments inside
Loosened teeth, or impaired sight,
    Whatever the need, physicians are there
    To grant peace of mind and expert care.

Do you need a tooth extracted
Are you suffering with pain in your back?
    Call your physician so he can help
    To ease the pain, or make you well.

Let us thank God for our physicians
Surgeons, neurologists, MDs, dentists,
    Because if it weren't for them
    We would suffer with unbearable pain.

God, we thank you for your creation
Of people of such devout dedication,
    Thank you, Lord, for our physicians
    Who keep us well in every season.

Giving Thanks for the Breath of Life

With so many expectant mothers today
For their unborn children tonight we pray,
 Because on that day, or delivery night
 God grants her baby His Breath of Life.

As we cherish each newborn child
God gives them a spirit oh so mild,
 Desiring to be held, loved and touched
 The Breath of life grants them so much.

Praise the Lord Jesus Christ
Who creates every precious life,
 Let him know how glad you are
 To have a soul, and a beating heart.

Thank you, Lord, for granting us life!
In our soul shines Your Holy Light.
 Thank you Lord, and may we live
 A life that's worthy of this gift!

Giving Thanks for Our Children

From the very first wail of life
Children bless us with their light.
> A beautiful innocence which they share
> With parents, strangers - anyone there.

Their first words, first steps, first loves
All remind us of how they need hugs.
> Arms outstretched, a smile that shines
> These little ones always need our time.

Let us give thanks for children, today
Boys and girls who brighten our way,
> With each memory we seal in our heart
> Each one becomes an important part.

Lord Jesus, thanks for our kids
Children of hope in whom you live,
> Thank you, Lord, for the joy they bring
> With a smile that makes the soul sing!

Giving Thanks for God's Wisdom

Day to day, in whatever we do
If we need it, all we need do,
    Is to ask the Lord for his wisdom
    And He will willingly bless you with it.

Have you ever felt at a loss?
All was bleak, no matter what?
    Then all of a sudden after you prayed
    From God's throne, your answer came!

God, our Father, is eternally wise
Desiring to grant us His insight,
    His wisdom is far beyond what we know
    But God wants his children to grow.

Thank You, Lord Father, for granting us
Your eternal, illuminating wisdom!
    Without it Lord, we'd be forever lost
    Thank You for your wisdom, dear God.

Giving Thanks for Our Freedom

Traveling from one place to another
Visiting a neighbor, sister, or mother,
    Saying whatever it is you believe-
    Men and women died so we could be free.

Simply attending your favorite church.
Here's a freedom: reading God's word!
    So many people can't do even that
    A freedom we so often take for granted.

Why, we are even free to read this verse
An act, that elsewhere, may be unheard.
    So on this day we bend our knees
    To thank our Lord for setting us free.

Father God, we lift up Your name
For setting us free in so many ways!
    Jesus Christ, you've done it again
    By setting us free from a lifetime of sin.

Giving Thanks for Our Health

Healthy, wealthy, wise these three
Are important to some, but not to me.
    Health and wisdom are most important
    If we are to know the heart of God.

Healthy bodies, healthy minds
Keep us in tune with Jesus Christ,
    That's not to say if you are blind or deaf
    In a wheelchair, you can't know God yet.

Thank you, God, for the health we have
To serve thee, and others, the handicapped,
    Our bodies are beautiful works of art
    Thank you from the depths of our hearts.

Robert S. Perkins

Giving Thanks for the Gospel

If it weren't for the gospel of Christ
We never would have known He was alive.
  Or of the life-giving gift he gave
  How our immortal souls could be saved.

We'd never have known of His healing touch
Or how much his Father loved us.
  But, hallelujah! The gospel is known!
  Now we know what Jesus has done.

He has promised til our dying day
That he will hear us when we pray,
  Most importantly, or so I've found
  He has saved us from being hell-bound.

Thank You, Lord, for granting to us
By the Gospel, the gift of Your love,
  Thank You, Lord, and may we be bold
  Enough to share your love with lost souls.

Giving Thanks for Therapists

I know you think this overlaps
With giving thanks for physicians
    But where physicians can't do it all
    Therapists quickly receive a call.

Working steadfastly with 'helpless' folk
Day after day, they work and hope,
    Exercising muscles that don't want to work
    Whether by stroke, strain, pull or worse.

Let us then give our thanks to God
For the therapists who work so hard
    To get us back in shape, once more
    So we can live our lives for the Lord.

Thank you, Lord, for therapists and aides
Working with us till we're back in shape,
    Thank you, Lord Jesus, for people who care
    As your healing touch they endeavor to share.

Giving Thanks for Missionaries

Dedicating their lives to their task
They share the gospel in a darkness so vast,
    With a hope in their heart wherever they go
    In their hometown or around the globe.

The images we create in our minds
Of missionaries is not that of Christ's,
    We envision them in tribal pots -
    How far off the mark we've gotten.

In deep forests, or frigid steeps
Dedicated people are called to preach,
    Leading lost souls who've never heard
    To Jesus Christ, by His Word.

Thank you, Lord God, for missionaries
Whose lives are spent in selfless caring,
    Thank you, Lord Jesus, we daily cry
    For those who lead us to your Light!

Giving Thanks for Our Technicians

If my TV were to blow a fuse
Melt down wires, whatever they do,
 When it decides to go and break down
 I call an electrician somewhere in town.

Automobiles are a high-tech mess
I won't touch them, cause I know less
 Than the neighbor guy living next door -
 I won't touch a modern day motor.

That's why God gave others the knowledge
To repair what I know I cannot.
 From repairing engines to flying spacecraft
 Technicians keep us all on track.

Thank you, Father, for our technicians
Who are blessed with your Wisdom,
 Thank you, Lord Jesus, for what they bring
 In to our lives - a form of you Peace.

Giving Thanks for Clothing and Food

Lord we thank Thee for this food
And the protection of clothes and shoes,
  Doesn't sound quite right, does it?
  But it makes us stop and think.

When was the last time you thanked God
For the clothing that protects your bod?
  Every day, or I hope we do
  We give God thanks for drinks and food.

Adam and Eve wore leaves of figs.
Today we wear anything we wish.
  The same thing goes for what we eat
  Hamburgers or salads, or anything gourmet.

We thank Thee, Lord, for clothing and food
Clearly a daily blessing from You.
  Thank you, Lord Jesus, for keeping us fed
  Until we stretch out in our beds.

Giving Thanks for the Ministry

In a day when we want to believe
But by Satan we are deceived,
    That's when we need to turn again
    To the devoted church of God men.

I'm not denouncing any denomination
I'm speaking of those in ministry.
    Elders, deacons, rabbis, priests
    Individuals God has called to preach.

Such individuals have various styles
It's what God uses to get the Word out.
    Thank God for the people He's called
    To teach, preach, and care for us all.

Father God, we thank You, today
For Your ministers who lead the way,
    Lord and Savior, we know it's hard
    So may we encourage each ministers heart.

Giving Thanks for Gravity

I'll fly away! Oh glory! I'll fly away!
We would fly away without gravity!
> This minor wonder which God created
> Keeps us anchored here, night and day.

Without that gravity we would float
About in the air like a listless boat.
> And those who sleep in bunk beds
> Would have bumps and bruises on their heads.

Yes, gravity is a wonderful blessing
Keeping us steadily on our feet.
> All jesting aside, there will come a day
> When we will all fly away.

Thank you, my Father, for gravity
Which for now keeps us chaos free.
> Thank you, Jesus, for this mystery of life
> Which keeps us all from taking flight.

Giving Thanks for Beautiful Flowers

From majestic roses to gold dandelion's
God has blessed the human eye.
    Like each individual human being
    No two flowers are exactly the same.

There's such a vast display of colors
And scents that sooth a angry heart,
    God created each flower for us
    So we may view a touch of His love.

Praise the Lord all the world 'round
For the beauty in flowers to be found.
    A gift of beauty that stirs the heart
    Or heals it by His loving Power.

Lord, we thank Thee for every bloom
That brightens our day, sweeps away gloom,
    Thank You, Jesus, for the beauty we see
    For it is a mirror image of Thee!

Giving Thanks for a Good Nights Rest

Say your boss has chewed you out?
You wife forgot you were taking her out?
    Did your tire on the way home, go flat?
    Then take God's hand and relax.

Has your day completely gone wrong?
Have been unable to sing a song?
    Are you weary? Do you feel unblessed?
    Then lay right back to sleep and to rest.

Oh I know you sometimes can't
With the children, the job, your mate,
    But every night when you go to bed
    The Lord is there to stroke your head.

Lord God, we thank You for every night
When we relax from our wild life,
    Lord Jesus Christ, as we drift into sleep
    Grant us, we pray, the rest we need.

Giving Thanks for Our Pets

They ask nothing except to be fed.
They love playing with the kids.
    They know when we are down or hurt
    They are always there as a comfort.

Pets bring us so much joy -
Just watch them play with girls and boys!
    Pets do more than just fetch our shoes
    They can bring out the best in you.

Cats, dogs, lizards, birds
Gerbals, mice, whatever they are.
    Give thanks to the Lord for every pet
    That shares with us His love just a bit.

Thank You, Lord God, for the pets we love
And for your Spirit that makes us one,
    Thank you, Jesus, for your smile
    Which pets bring around when we are down.

Giving Thanks for Medication

Physicians, therapists, medication
All three go together any day!
    The third part of that equation
    Help's us remain well, day after day.

As an epileptic, I must take pills
To keep me from seizures, or being ill,
    My charming wife, who has MS
    Takes medicine so it won't get any worse.

God has blessed us with medicine
To hopefully make us well again,
    Should you have CP, diabetes
    Thank the Lord for the medicine you take.

Thank you, Lord, for medication
Which we take to remain well,
    Thank You, Lord Jesus, for our elation
    For keeping us well through our medication.

Giving Thanks for Mom and Dad

They love us, they keep us
They clothe us, they keep us.
They teach us, we love them
We need our Dad and our Mom.

Who else could rear us right?
They were there on scary, dark nights.
Mom and Dad took us to church
Introducing us to God's holy Word.

They help us get started on our own.
Two better friends have never been known -
Til our Lord we finally face
For Mom and Dad, let us give thanks.

Lord, we pray this Thanksgiving day
For Mom's and Dad's, bless them we pray!
Keep them, Jesus, close to your heart
Thank you, Lord, for our Mothers and Fathers.

Giving Thanks for Our Veterans

They fought for you
They fought for me,
    They fought for truth
    And our liberty.

Veteran men, and women too
Continue to fight for me and you,
    Suffering casualties, sometime loss
    Fighting for freedom; moralities cause.

Army. Navy. Air Force. Marine.
Not forgetting the ROTC!
    Thanking the Lord for our veterans
    Who fought and died for our freedom.

Lord Father, you know what it's like
To lose Your Son in a battlefield fight,
    Jesus Christ, You fought and You won
    Becoming for us the Veteran of Love.

Giving Thanks for the Gift of Prayer

When a child kneels down to pray
They thank God for Mommy and Daddy.
 When adults go to the Lord
 They thank Him for so much more.

Prayer is a way to communicate
With our Maker; to give Him praise,
 Or, if you will, to send Him a letter
 A verbal 'postcard' to our creator.

Thank the Lord for this gift
That brings us so much closer to Him,
 Pray for thanksgiving, or forgiveness.
 Pray for His will, if you are His.

Thank You, Lord, for letting us bring
To Your throne our every need,
 Thank You, Jesus, for hearing our prayers
 Proof in itself that You really do care.

Giving Thanks for Our Tears

Sliding down our cheeks and chin
Tears bring healing to pains within.
　　Releasing tension, easing strife
　　Bringing perspective to our life.

Jesus cried tears of pain
Knowing He had to die the next day.
　　Shedding His tears for sinful mankind
　　Tears of compassion flowed from His eyes.

When a loved one is lost in death
We find release when tears are wept,
　　Yes, tears are a blessing in disguise
　　Which God has given these mortal eyes.

Thank You, Lord, for tears we weep
Finding their home at Jesus' feet,
　　Thank You, Jesus, for weeping for us
　　Glorious tears that were shed in love.

Giving Thanks for Christmas

For the long trek to Bethlehem.
For the shepherds who heard and came.
    For the angelic choir who sang.
    We give You thanks for all of them.

For shedding Your robes to be born
In a manger, a feeding trough.
    For growing up in a carpenters shop
    We thank You, precious Lord of lords.

For coming to earth to take away sin.
For healing bodies, without and within.
    For touching our lives, being a part
    We thank You Lord for a whole new start.

Lord our God, Father of all
Thank You for sending Your Son, most of all.
    Lord Jesus Christ, light of our souls
    Thank You for setting aside Your robes.

Giving Thanks for Easter Day

Three short years to touch our lives
Even granting sight to the blind,
　　One last act must be made in love
　　The crucifixion of Jehovah's son!

Part Two of the story of Christ
Is a stone rolled away - He is ALIVE!
　　The Saviour who gave life to the dead
　　Has been miraculously resurrected!

Part Three: He has ascended to Glory
But that doesn't end the story -
　　Someday He is coming again
　　To judge the hearts and souls of men.

Heavenly Father, let Your praises ring
For the Easter Day King of kings!
　　Thank You, Jesus, for Easter Day
　　When You conquered sin, death, and Satan.

Giving Thanks for Thanksgiving

Sounds a little redundant? Maybe so.
Give thanks for thanksgiving even so.
> What do you have to give thanks for?
> Look around, there are reasons galore!

The stars, the air, the sun, the moon
Your sight, smell, and fingertips too.
> Thanking God for all we have
> Is the best gift He's ever had.

Yes, thanksgiving goes beyond Plymouth
Further back than Calvary, even.
> Thanksgiving originated back in Eden
> For God's creation of everything.

Thank You, Lord God, as we pray
We thank You for our nights and days,
> Thank You, Jesus, for creating man
> In love we give thee Thanksgiving. AMEN.

Giving Thanks for Memories

On a cool and dreary night
Memories can warm the heart up right,
    Of beloved children as they've grown
    Or a vacation spot to which you've flown.

Summer nights while at a dance
Can conjure up memories of romance,
    Of opening packages every Yule
    And many have memories of Sunday School.

You can't forget your wedding day
Or the day on which you were Saved!
    Memories can blow away our blues
    If we'll remember but one or two.

Thank You, Father, for the memories
That bring us joy, fill us with peace.
    Thank You, Jesus, for memories of us
    Which bring You warmth, joy and love.

Giving Thanks for the Lord Our God

For all the reasons of which to give thanks
There's only one reason we're here today,
    God saw fit to create each soul
    Each heart, each mind, individually whole.

God-the greatest mystery to man
Who shared with us salvation's plan,
    God who lives in Heaven, somewhere
    All at once can hear millions of prayers.

He desires to be our Father Superior
Even though we are sinfully inferior,
    God is the reason we lift our praise
    On Thanksgiving and every day.

Father God, we thank You for You
For being there when we are blue,
    Jesus, we thank You for making it
    Simpler to meet our Maker.

Giving Thanks for a Home Church

Where we find shelter, comfort, peace
Fellowship, joy, a Christian family,
    All are found in a place of worship
    Otherwise known as the family church.

Not just a building of brick and stone
The church, in fact, is God's home,
    Though our hearts are His resting place
    The church is where we bring Him praise.

Weddings, sermons, baptisms, revivals,
God's church ought to be sanctified.
    Let us thank God, for this day
    For His church, and unending grace.

Thank You, Father, for Your church
Where, in our hearts, Your Spirit works,
    Thank You, Jesus, for all You teach
    Through the ones You've called to preach.

Giving Thanks for Transportation

Planes, trains, automobiles,
Buses, buggies, bicycles -
    Many more modes of transportation
    Get us to meetings or vacations.

Motorcycles make our life a breeze
If we're not stopped by the police!
    Local buses take us to the mall
    Or, if it's in range, to City Hall.

Miracles with motors, that's what they are
From semi-trailers to Porsch sports cars,
    Let us give thanks for the knowledge He gave
    To create the first car, on that fateful day.

Heavenly Father, thank You, again
For the Wisdom You impart to men,
    Jesus Christ, we give you the praise
    For the blessings of transportation.